CONTENTS

Quatre Motets
pour le temps de Noël

Francis Poulenc
(1899–1963)

For mixed chorus a cappella.

Composed: 1951–52

Duration: approximately 11 minutes

Poulenc was born into a wealthy bourgeois household in Paris. He began playing piano at age five, encouraged by his mother, an amateur pianist who came from a family of artists. His father, the director of a successful pharmaceutical business, requested that Francis receive a traditional education before entering in the conservatory. Poulenc was left to follow the path of his choosing, however, as his parents both passed away before he turned nineteen. In 1914, he began studying composition with Ricardo Viñes. Not only did Viñes premiere many of Poulenc's works, he also acted as a spiritual guide for the fledgling musician. Poulenc credited Viñes with his embarking on a career as a performer and composer, and with introducing him to important contemporary composers of the time such as Auric, Satie, and Falla. Poulenc was deeply embedded in artistic and intellectual Parisian circles. He dedicated his first work, *Rapsodie nègre*, to Satie and Stravinsky recommended his music to Chester publishing house in London. In addition, his works were performed alongside those of Milhaud, Aric, Honegger, Tailleferre, and Durey at the studio of the painter Emile Lejeune. These gatherings led to the founding of "Les Six" in 1920, a group of composers whose friendship was strong despite variance in the aesthetics of their works. For long periods of his life, Pouluenc was a devout Catholic, and his faith was a central theme in many of his works. His works span multiple genres, including the operas *Les mammelles de Tirésias*, *La voix humaine* and *Dialogues des carmélites*, concertos, 150 art songs, chamber music, piano music and choral works, including the oratorio *Gloria*.

Quatre motets pour le temps de Noël was completed in 1952. Poulenc often returned to traditional forms of French church music popular in the Renaissance, such as the motet, that had fallen out of favor in the late eighteenth century. According to Poulenc biographer Benjamin Ivry, the four vivid motets are "the product of a composer who has studied hundred of religious paintings, and who tried to evoke some landscapes in his writing for voices."[1] Following the narrative of the Nativity, Poulenc intended that the movements be performed together. However, there is a long history of them being performed separately.

O magnum mysterium

"O magnum mysterium" is a responsorial chant traditionally recanted during the Christmas Matins, the monastic nighttime liturgy that ends at dawn. It depicts the stable following Christ's birth in quiet period of reprieve before its news is proclaimed to the shepherds. Poulenc dedicated this movement to his friend, the Dutch pianist and conductor Félix de Nobel.

O magnum mysterium,,	*O great mystery*
et admirabile sacramentum,	*and wonderful sacrament*
ut animalia víderent Dominum natum,	*that animals should see the newborn Lord,*
jacentem in præsepio.	*lying in a manger.*
Beata Virgo cujus viscera	*Blessed virgin, whose womb*
meruerunt portare	*was worthy to carry*
Dominum Christum.	*Christ the Lord.*

Quem vidistis pastores dicite

"Quem vidistis pastores dicite" recalls the message given to the shepherds of the Savior's birth. The text is the third responsorial chant for the Matins on Christmas Day. Poulenc dedicated the movement to his friend and confidant Simone Girard.

Quem vidistis, pastores, dicite,	*Who have you seen, shepherds, tell us,*
annunciate nobis,	*announce to us,*
in terris quis apparuit?	*who has appeared on earth?*
Natum vidimus et choros angelorum	*We saw the newborn and the choirs of angels*
collaudantes Dominum.	*praising the Lord.*
Dicite, quidnam vidistis?	*Say, what did you see?*
et annuntiate Christi nativitatem.	*and announce the birth of Christ.*

Videntes stellam

The text of "Videntes stellam," a responsory for the Christmas Matins, paints a picture of the star in the sky that leads the Magi to Christ. This movement is dedicated to Madeleine Bataille.

Videntes stellam magi	*Seeing the star, the wise men*
gavisi sunt gaudio magno:	*rejoiced with great joy;*
et intrantes domum,	*and entering the house,*
obtulerunt Domino	*they offered the Lord*
aurum, thus et myrrham.	*gold, frankincense and myrrh.*

Hodie Christus natus est

"Hodie Christus natus est" is an Antiphon to the Magnificat, which is sung during the vespers on Christmas Day. Here the text speaks of the world rejoicing together over the birth of Christ. Poulenc dedicated this movement to the French conductor Marcel Couraud.

Hodie Christus natus est:	*Today Christ is born;*
hodie salvator apparuit:	*today the savior has appeared;*
Hodie in terra canunt angeli,	*today on earth the angels sing,*
laetantur archangeli:	*the archangels rejoice;*
Hodie exultant justi, dicentes:	*today the just exult, saying:*
gloria in excelsis Deo, alleluia	*glory in the highest to God, alleluia*

[1]Benjamin Ivry, *Francis Poulenc* (London: Phaidon Press Limited, 1996), 162.

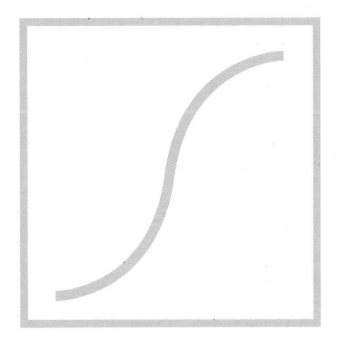

SALABERT

à Félix de Nobel

I. O MAGNUM MYSTERIUM

5ᵉ répons des matines de Noël

pour chœur a cappella

Francis Poulenc

O MAGNUM MYSTERIUM

O MAGNUM MYSTERIUM

Noizay, avril 1952

à Simone Girard

II. QUEM VIDISTIS, PASTORES DICITE

3ᵉ répons des matines de Noël

pour chœur a cappella

Francis Poulenc

- res? di - ci - te, an - nun tia - te no - bis in ter - ris quis ap - pa - ru- it?

Na - tum vi - di - mus et cho - ros An - ge - lo - rum

Na - tum vi - di - mus cho - ros An - ge - lo - rum

Na - tum vi - di - mus et cho - ros An - ge - lo - rum

QUEM VIDISTIS PASTORES DICITE

QUEM VIDISTIS PASTORES DICITE

QUEM VIDISTIS PASTORES DICITE

QUEM VIDISTIS PASTORES DICITE

QUEM VIDISTIS PASTORES DICITE

QUEM VIDISTIS PASTORES DICITE

Marseille, décembre 1951

à Madeleine Bataille

III. VIDENTES STELLAM

Antienne de Magnificat (octave de l'Epiphanie 2ᵉ jour)

pour chœur a cappella

Francis Poulenc

© 1952 by Rouart, Lerolle
© Éditions SALABERT
Paris, France

VIDENTES STELLAM

VIDENTES STELLAM

VIDENTES STELLAM   Aix en Provence, novembre 1951

à Marcel Couraud

IV. HODIE CHRISTUS NATUS EST
Antienne du Magnificat des 2e Vêpres de Noël
pour chœur a cappella

Francis Poulenc

HODIE CHRISTUS NATUS EST

HODIE CHRISTUS NATUS EST

HODIE CHRISTUS NATUS EST

HODIE CHRISTUS NATUS EST

HODIE CHRISTUS NATUS EST

42

44